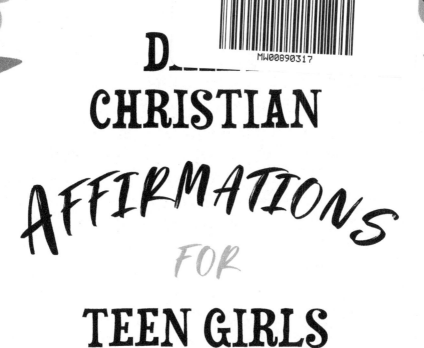

D̲̲̲̲̲̲̲
CHRISTIAN

AFFIRMATIONS

FOR

TEEN GIRLS

365
ENCOURAGING
BIBLE VERSES FOR
YOUNG WOMEN

MADE
EASY
PRESS

Producer & International Distributor
eBookPro Publishing
www.ebook-pro.com

DAILY CHRISTIAN AFFIRMATIONS FOR TEEN GIRLS
Encouraging Bible Verses for Young Women

Made Easy Press

Contact: agency@ebook-pro.com

ISBN 9798865353379

This book belongs to

....

Introduction

Navigating the world as a teenage girl is a challenge. There's a lot to deal with, like school, extracurricular activities, chores, friends, romantic relationships, and physical changes, all while growing up and figuring yourself out as a person.

It can be overwhelming, and you might sometimes feel that it's all too much.

But God's Word can help you get through anything – even the challenging teenage years.

This little book is a well of encouragement, inspiration, and wisdom, to boost your confidence through a whole year.

Every day for 52 weeks, Monday through Sunday, you will find an empowering affirmation reminding you just how strong, brave, capable, and beautiful you are, and of all the wonderful things God has in store for you!

And the best thing is – you can start right away, next Monday!

Keep this book by your bed or on your desk, somewhere close at hand, and clear two minutes each morning to start the day with a confidence-boosting, thought-provoking dose of self-love.

YOU'VE GOT THIS!

Day 1:

Monday

I will take the time to appreciate
quiet moments this morning.

Day 2:

Tuesday

I follow Jesus no matter
where he leads me.

Day 3:

Wednesday

I am beautiful by God's definition.

Day 4:

Thursday

I can do anything I put my mind to.

Day **5:**

Friday

I am creatively inspired
by the world around me.

Day **6:**

Saturday

I have the power to thrive.

Day **7:**

Sunday

Positivity is a choice
that I choose to make.

Day **8:**

Monday

I am excited to take in new experiences
and gain knowledge.

Day **9:**

Tuesday

I can handle anything life throws at me.

Day **10:**

Wednesday

I am confident in the presence of others.

Day **11:**

Thursday

I love all of God's creatures,
including people, animals, and plants.

Day 12:

Friday

When I feel overwhelmed,
I cry out to God and find safety.

Day 13:

Saturday

I put God first in my life.

Day 14:

Sunday

God has exceptional things
in store for me.

Day 15:

Monday

I will find God when I seek him
with all of my heart.

Day 16:

Tuesday

I am a role model to my siblings,

cousins, and friends.

Day 17:

Wednesday

My hard work will pay off.

Day 18:

Thursday

I don't need anyone else
to tell me I am worthy.

Day **19**:

Friday

I am a good person who deserves
happiness, health, and peace.

Day **20**:

Saturday

I am capable of making positive choices
that lead me to what I want.

Day **21**:

Sunday

I have friends who love me.

Day 22:

Monday

I guard my heart because it
determines the course of my life.

Day 23:

Tuesday

Nothing can stop me
from achieving my dreams.

Day 24:

Wednesday

There is so much for me
to see and experience.

Day 25:

Thursday

I am in harmony and balance with life.

Day 26:

Friday

I am wonderfully made.

Day 27:

Saturday

Success is within my reach.

Day 28:

Sunday

I am in charge of how I feel
and I choose to feel happy.

Day **29:**
Monday

I have my own sense of style
and it is unique.

Day **30:**
Tuesday

I have the peace of Christ.

Day **31:**
Wednesday

I focus on the positive things in my life.

Day **32:**
Thursday

No one else in the world is like me.

Day 33:

Friday

I am grateful for everything that I have.

Day 34:

Saturday

I am creative.

Day 35:

Sunday

It's okay to be sad sometimes.

Week 6

Day **36:**

Monday

I am faithful.

Day **37:**

Tuesday

I get to decide what is best for me.

Day **38:**

Wednesday

There are people I haven't met yet
who will become an important part of my life.

Day **39:**

Thursday

I live with kindness.

Day **40**:
Friday

I persevere.

Day **41**:
Saturday

I am loved just as I am.

Day **42**:
Sunday

Other people's words
cannot hurt me.

Day **43:**

Monday

My prayers will be answered by God.

Day **44:**

Tuesday

I can find joy even in the smallest things.

Day **45:**

Wednesday

I can rely on God.

Day **46:**

Thursday

I am becoming closer to
my true self every day.

Friday

I can have wisdom and guidance
from God if I just ask.

Saturday

I am peaceful and whole.

Sunday

I take the time to appreciate
the beautiful things I see.

Week 8

Day **50**:

Monday

I am created in God's image.

Day **51**:

Tuesday

I appreciate all the gifts I have received.

Day **52**:

Wednesday

My flaws are a part of me
and I embrace them.

Day **53**:

Thursday

I am fortunate.

Day 54:

Friday

I am beautiful, smart and talented.

Day 55:

Saturday

God is my strength and shield.

Day 56:

Sunday

God gives me strength.

Week 9

Day 57:
Monday

God loves those who love him.

Day 58:
Tuesday

I have sound knowledge and wisdom.

Day 59:
Wednesday

I am happy where I am in my life
right now.

Day 60:
Thursday

I appreciate the body that God gave me.

Day **61:**

Friday

I have the courage to do
challenging things.

Day **62:**

Saturday

I am a unique gift to the world.

Day **63:**

Sunday

I become a better version
of myself every day.

Day 64:

Monday

I deflect negativity.

Day 65:

Tuesday

I acknowledge that there is
a time and a place for everything.

Day 66:

Wednesday

God chose me to be His.

Day 67:

Thursday

I did the best that I could
at the moment.

Day **68:**

Friday

I have everything I need to succeed.

Day **69:**

Saturday

I am at peace with
who I am as a person.

Day **70:**

Sunday

I am Jesus Christ's friend.

Day 71:

Monday

As I place my hope in the Lord,
my strength is renewed.

Day 72:

Tuesday

I enjoy helping others.

Day 73:

Wednesday

I won't settle for less than I deserve.

Day 74:

Thursday

I can do hard things.

Day 75:

Friday

God is looking after me.

Day 76:

Saturday

I don't have to spend time
with people who make me feel bad.

Day 77:

Sunday

God is with me.

Week 12

Day 78:
Monday

I channel my anger into healthy outlets.

Day 79:
Tuesday

I look for the good in each day.

Day 80:
Wednesday

I am bold in my actions.

Day 81:
Thursday

God is my refuge.

Day **82:**

Friday

I let go of all negative emotions and fear.

Day **83:**

Saturday

I have meaningful and equal relationships
with my friends and family.

Day **84:**

Sunday

My trust lies in God alone.

Day 85:

Monday

The more I like myself,
the more others will like me.

Day 86:

Tuesday

My life is filled with beauty and grace.

Day 87:

Wednesday

I am surrounded by positive
and supportive people.

Day 88:

Thursday

I strive for improvement,
not for perfection.

30

Day **89:**

Friday

God guides me with love.

Day **90:**

Saturday

I can show my devotion to God
by loving everyone.

Day **91:**

Sunday

I respect my body for the
unique way it is made.

Week 14

Day 92:
Monday

I am beautiful both inside and out.

Day 93:
Tuesday

In ten years, I will be exactly
where I want to be.

Day 94:
Wednesday

I forgive myself for past mistakes.

Day 95:
Thursday

I am open to limitless possibilities.

Day **96:**

Friday

How other people talk or act
doesn't reflect on me.

Day **97:**

Saturday

I am grateful for all that
God has given me.

Day **98:**

Sunday

I may be young, but that doesn't
mean I don't have worth.

Day 99:
Monday

My mistakes don't define me.

Day 100:
Tuesday

My voice matters.

Day 101:
Wednesday

Challenges are what make my life interesting.

Day 102:
Thursday

I have countless skills and talents.

Day **103**:

Friday

I don't need to follow along
with what everyone else is doing.

Day **104**:

Saturday

I have might and power.

Day **105**:

Sunday

I am smart.

Day **106:**

Monday

I belong where I am.

Day **107:**

Tuesday

I am kind to people and animals.

Day **108:**

Wednesday

There is no one else in the world
who is exactly like me.

Day **109:**

Thursday

I am blessed.

Day **110**:

Friday

I make time to care for myself.

Day **111**:

Saturday

I am sensitive and human.

Day **112**:

Sunday

I am a light that
shines on the world.

37

Day 113:

Monday

I am allowed to ask for
what I want and what I need.

Day 114:

Tuesday

I have all that I need.

Day 115:

Wednesday

I rise above gossip and
talking rudely about others.

Day 116:

Thursday

My body is beautiful just the way it is.

Day 117:

Friday

Each day is a blessing and a gift.

Day 118:

Saturday

I honor my parents
and do what they ask of me.

Day 119:

Sunday

There is nothing too hard for God.

Day 120:

Monday

It is enough to do my best.

Day 121:

Tuesday

I am patient.

Day 122:

Wednesday

Today is going to be a really,
really great day.

Day 123:

Thursday

I learn from each relationship,
even if it doesn't work out.

Day **124:**
Friday

No one in the world is perfect.

Day **125:**
Saturday

I make good choices.

Day **126:**
Sunday

God knows my deepest
thoughts and hopes.

Day **127:**

Monday

God will supply all my needs.

Day **128:**

Tuesday

I am not afraid to work hard.

Day **129:**

Wednesday

It's okay that I have different
interests than my friends.

Day **130:**

Thursday

I am on an adventure
to discover myself.

42

Day **131**:

Friday

I speak with love.

Day **132**:

Saturday

God fights for me.

Day **133**:

Sunday

God woke me up this morning
for a purpose.

Day **134:**

Monday

I have hobbies and interests of my own.

Day **135:**

Tuesday

I am responsible for myself.

Day **136:**

Wednesday

Life does not have to be perfect
to be wonderful.

Day **137:**

Thursday

I have confidence in God's power.

Day 138:

Friday

I have goals and dreams
that I am going to achieve.

Day 139:

Saturday

My head is full of new ideas.

Day 140:

Sunday

I choose hope.

Day 141:

Monday

It's okay for me to have fun.

Day 142:

Tuesday

My roots teach me who I am.

Day 143:

Wednesday

I am enough.

Day 144:

Thursday

I am God's beloved daughter.

Day **145**:

Friday

Everything about me is intentionally
designed by God.

Day **146**:

Saturday

I can choose to do things
differently from others.

Day **147**:

Sunday

I love who I am right now.

Day 148:
Monday

God's Spirit makes me feel powerful.

Day 149:
Tuesday

I am learning to love myself
the way God does.

Day 150:
Wednesday

I will not worry about the future.

Day 151:
Thursday

I appreciate myself for all I do.

Day 152:

Friday

God's power works best
in my weakness.

Day 153:

Saturday

I appreciate the life that God gave me.

Day 154:

Sunday

Wonderful things are going
to happen to me.

Day 155:

Monday

I am open and honest with my feelings.

Day 156:

Tuesday

I appreciate every creation of God.

Day 157:

Wednesday

"Normal" isn't real.
I am unique and that is beautiful.

Day 158:

Thursday

It's okay to admit when I am wrong
and to ask for forgiveness.

Day 159:
Friday

God does not forsake
those who seek Him.

Day 160:
Saturday

I care about the environment.

Day 161:
Sunday

I am healthy.

Day 162:
Monday

I can forgive myself.

Day 163:
Tuesday

My faith makes me whole.

Day 164:
Wednesday

I am a good and caring friend.

Day 165:
Thursday

I have a community that cares about me.

Day 166:

Friday

Language is powerful.
I choose the words I say carefully.

Day 167:

Saturday

I am open to receiving advice
from people with more wisdom than me.

Day 168:

Sunday

I am keeping my body
safe and healthy.

Day 169:

Monday

I am happy to be alive.

Day 170:

Tuesday

I am safe in God's care.

Day 171:

Wednesday

My feelings deserve recognition.

Day 172:

Thursday

I am a good, law-abiding citizen.

Day 173:

Friday

I am a woman of discipline
and self-control.

Day 174:

Saturday

I stand up for myself
because I matter.

Day 175:

Sunday

I trust myself to make
the right decision.

Week 26

Day 176:

Monday

I am loved by God.

Day 177:

Tuesday

I am part of God's huge family.

Day 178:

Wednesday

I don't have to be the center of attention.

Day 179:

Thursday

I can change the world.

Day **180**:

Friday

I am whole and complete.

Day **181**:

Saturday

God is always with me.

Day **182**:

Sunday

I am content.

Day 183:

Monday

I can talk to God about anything.

Day 184:

Tuesday

My first love will probably not be
my only love, and that's okay.

Day 185:

Wednesday

I live in the moment.

Day 186:

Thursday

There will always be bumps in the road.

Day **187**:

Friday

I am my own best friend.

Day **188**:

Saturday

God listens to me.

Day **189**:

Sunday

God will give me the strength I need to do
everything He wants me to do today.

Day 190:

Monday

I am in control of my thoughts.

Day 191:

Tuesday

I am beautiful.

Day 192:

Wednesday

Simple things can make me happy.

Day 193:

Thursday

I am important to so many people.

Day 194:

Friday

I will do great things.

Day 195:

Saturday

I accept myself for who I am.

Day 196:

Sunday

I am not too much for God to handle.

Day 197:

Monday

My trust is in the Lord.

Day 198:

Tuesday

There's always something
new for me to learn.

Day 199:

Wednesday

I am doing a great job growing up.

Day 200:

Thursday

I make choices that honor my body.

Day 201:
Friday

If I ever struggle, I have people
who will help me.

Day 202:
Saturday

God will never leave or forsake me.

Day 203:
Sunday

I live in the present.

Day 204:
Monday

I keep my online posting
positive and affirming.

Day 205:
Tuesday

I am capable of unconditional love.

Day 206:
Wednesday

I can control how I respond
to things that bother me.

Day 207:
Thursday

I have confidence that I can do
all things through Christ.

Day 208:

Friday

Challenges make me
stronger and wiser.

Day 209:

Saturday

I am willing to ask for what I need.

Day 210:

Sunday

I am responsible
with my technology.

Day **211:**

Monday

I put my energy into things
that matter to me.

Day **212:**

Tuesday

I know how to be still
so I can hear from God.

Day **213:**

Wednesday

My prayers are heard.

Day **214:**

Thursday

I am empowered to shut down
conversations I am uncomfortable with
or that may hurt other people.

Day 215:

Friday

I trust God wholeheartedly.

Day 216:

Saturday

I like the person I am becoming.

Day 217:

Sunday

I am absolutely unique.

Day 218:

Monday

I don't owe all of my time to anyone.

Day 219:

Tuesday

I am complete as I am.

Day 220:

Wednesday

I let go of regret.

Day 221:

Thursday

I am a worthy child of God.

Day 222:

Friday

I do what I can.

Day 223:

Saturday

My confidence grows when I step
outside my comfort zone.

Day 224:

Sunday

My heart is open to all of the wisdom
the world has to offer.

Day **225**:
Monday

If I mess up today,
I can try again tomorrow.

Day **226**:
Tuesday

I am empowered to be
the best version of myself.

Day **227**:
Wednesday

God is my stronghold in times of trouble.

Day **228**:
Thursday

I look forward to tomorrow
and the opportunities that await me.

Day **229**:

Friday

Today, I will do something
that scares me.

Day **230**:

Saturday

I am boundlessly strong
as God is with me.

Day **231**:

Sunday

I am capable of changing my mind
when presented with new information.

Day 232:

Monday

I am a little weird but so is everyone.

Day 233:

Tuesday

It's okay to make mistakes.

Day 234:

Wednesday

More people care about me
than I even know.

Day 235:

Thursday

I love and respect my family
for all they do for me.

Day 236:

Friday

Everything will work out for me.

Day 237:

Saturday

My mind is full of brilliant ideas

Day 238:

Sunday

I represent the values that matter
to me and my community.

Day 239:

Monday

God wants me to be happy.

Day 240:

Tuesday

I am a living, breathing miracle.

Day 241:

Wednesday

The people who judge me are the people
who are most afraid of being judged.

Day 242:

Thursday

I am free from expectations and criticism.

Day 243:

Friday

I learn from the word of God.

Day 244:

Saturday

I have a bright future ahead of me.

Day 245:

Sunday

I am optimistic because
today is a new day.

Week 36

Day 246:
Monday

I deserve to be surrounded
by people I love.

Day 247:
Tuesday

I have a positive mindset.

Day 248:
Wednesday

I am enough.

Day 249:
Thursday

Good things await me.

Day **250**:
Friday

My mind is clear.

Day **251**:
Saturday

My body is my own.

Day **252**:
Sunday

I take things one day at a time.

Day **253:**

Monday

Every day is a fresh start.

Day **254:**

Tuesday

I can tell my own story.

Day **255:**

Wednesday

I am open to new ways
of improving myself.

Day **256:**

Thursday

I am grateful for each breath
God gives me.

Day **257:**

Friday

I am a work of art.

Day **258:**

Saturday

I take pride in my ability to make
worthwhile contributions to the world.

Day **259:**

Sunday

I live every day to the fullest.

Day 260:
Monday

I am smart, but I don't know everything.

Day 261:
Tuesday

I can be soft in my heart
and firm in my boundaries.

Day 262:
Wednesday

Changing my mind is a strength,
not a weakness.

Day 263:
Thursday

I will do better next time.

Day 264:

Friday

Today I focus on God
to fill me with peace of mind.

Day 265:

Saturday

I care about what is going on
in the world.

Day 266:

Sunday

God is right here with me,
holding my hand.

Day 267:

Monday

With faith I am able to move mountains.

Day 268:

Tuesday

I embrace change
and rise to new opportunities.

Day 269:

Wednesday

I am the hero of my own story.

Day 270:

Thursday

I don't have to please anyone
other than myself.

Day **271**:

Friday

The people I see on Instagram
are not perfect.

Day **272**:

Saturday

I will respect myself and others because
we are all made in the image of God.

Day **273**:

Sunday

I am walking in the wisdom of God.

Day 274:

Monday

Happiness is within my grasp.

Day 275:

Tuesday

Saying "no" makes me stronger.

Day 276:

Wednesday

I stand up for what I believe in.

Day 277:

Thursday

I live by faith.

Day **278**:

Friday

God has great plans for my life.

Day **279**:

Saturday

To show love to God,
I show love to myself.

Day **280**:

Sunday

In five years, it will not matter
what I wore today.

Day **281:**

Monday

I let go of grudges.

Day **282:**

Tuesday

The Lord hears me
and answers me when I call Him.

Day **283:**

Wednesday

I release the pressure to excel.

Day **284:**

Thursday

God loves me with everlasting love.

Day 285:

Friday

I will acknowledge God
in all of my ways.

Day 286:

Saturday

I choose Godly things.

Day 287:

Sunday

I have a family that loves me.

Week 42

Day 288:

Monday

It's okay to be proud of myself
and my accomplishments.

Day 289:

Tuesday

Today will be a day to remember.

Day 290:

Wednesday

I have a constant source of truth
in God's word.

Day 291:

Thursday

I believe in myself as God believes in me.

Day 292:

Friday

I am kind and respectful to the elderly.

Day 293:

Saturday

I do not have to compare myself
to anyone else.

Day 294:

Sunday

I am everything God says I am.

Day **295:**

Monday

I am valued and helpful.

Day **296:**

Tuesday

I am loved by God
more than I can imagine.

Day **297:**

Wednesday

I am held and supported
by those who love me.

Day **298:**

Thursday

I am accepted by God.

Day **299**:

Friday

Even my wildest dreams can come true.

Day **300**:

Saturday

God is looking out for me.

Day **301**:

Sunday

I don't need likes and comments
to be fulfilled.

Day **302:**
Monday

My future is mine to choose.

Day **303:**
Tuesday

Just because I haven't reached my destination
doesn't mean that I am lost.

Day **304:**
Wednesday

I deserve a loving and equal
romantic relationship.

Day **305:**
Thursday

I am learning valuable lessons
from myself every day.

Day 306:

Friday

I am saved.

Day 307:

Saturday

I have control over
my thoughts and words.

Day 308:

Sunday

I have the power
to face any difficulty.

Day **309**:

Monday

I am God's precious child.

Day **310**:

Tuesday

Fear has no place in my life.

Day **311**:

Wednesday

I am relaxed and happy with where I am.

Day **312**:

Thursday

I do not pretend to be anyone
or anything other than who I am.

Day **313:**

Friday

I don't have to participate
if I don't want to.

Day **314:**

Saturday

Growing up is an adventure.

Day **315:**

Sunday

God's faithfulness is new
every morning.

Day 316:

Monday

I am focused on what matters most.

Day 317:

Tuesday

I am true to myself.

Day 318:

Wednesday

I am growing up at my own pace.

Day 319:

Thursday

I am a loving being.

Day 320:

Friday

Trying new things
opens new opportunities.

Day 321:

Saturday

My light cannot be extinguished.

Day 322:

Sunday

I may not have all the answers,
and I am okay with that.

Day **323:**
Monday

My worth is defined by His grace.

Day **324:**
Tuesday

I love with my whole heart.

Day **325:**
Wednesday

I radiate confidence.

Day **326:**
Thursday

I deserve the healthiest version of myself.

98

Day 327:
Friday

I trust that I am on the right path.

Day 328:
Saturday

I do not need drugs or alcohol
to have fun.

Day 329:
Sunday

My opinions are unique and important.

Week 48

Day 330:
Monday

My life is not a race or a competition.

Day 331:
Tuesday

I trust God at all times.

Day 332:
Wednesday

All my problems have solutions.

Day 333:
Thursday

My focus is sharp.

Day **334:**
Friday

As God was with Moses,
He will also be with me.

Day **335:**
Saturday

I deserve to be happy.

Day **336:**
Sunday

Every storm will pass.

Day **337**:

Monday

I do not have to reveal my whole self
on social media.

Day **338**:

Tuesday

I am allowed to feel good.

Day **339**:

Wednesday

I understand that my actions become habits,
so I will try to do the right thing.

Day **340**:

Thursday

God wants me to live.

Day **341:**

Friday

I invite art, music, and beauty
into my life.

Day **342:**

Saturday

I will commit my way to God
and trust in Him.

Day **343:**

Sunday

I have big dreams.

Day **344**:

Monday

I am proud of who I am.

Day **345**:

Tuesday

I am lucky to have the
opportunities that I do.

Day **346**:

Wednesday

I celebrate the good qualities
in others and myself.

Day **347**:

Thursday

I am never alone.

Day 348:
Friday

I uplift the people around me.

Day 349:
Saturday

My life is a gift.

Day 350:
Sunday

It's okay to be scared sometimes.

Day **351:**
Monday

I am willing to accept help when offered.

Day **352:**
Tuesday

I breathe in positivity and
exhale negative thinking.

Day **353:**
Wednesday

Right now, I am exactly
what God created me to be.

Day **354:**
Thursday

I am fearless.

Day **355:**

Friday

God's approval of me is most important.

Day **356:**

Saturday

My sorrows will be turned into joy.

Day **357:**

Sunday

I deserve friends that treat me
with equal love and kindness.

Day 358:

Monday

I am capable of being responsible for myself.

Day 359:

Tuesday

God has good plans for me.

Day 360:

Wednesday

I face each challenge with grace.

Day 361:

Thursday

I can clearly express to others
when I feel hurt.

Day **362**:
Friday

Today I will learn and grow.

Day **363**:
Saturday

I am good and getting better.

Day **364**:
Sunday

Jesus Christ is my friend.

Day 365:

Monday

I can turn every ending
into a wonderful new beginning.

Thank you so much for reading Daily Christian
Affirmations for Teen Girls!

It means the world to us to be able to bring girls just
like you everywhere closer to their faith.

I hope you enjoyed your journey and feel
empowered and blessed.

We'd appreciate it so much if you would consider
going to Amazon and leaving a review.

Your reviews help us bring you more beautiful and
meaningful content like this book.

About Made Easy Press

At Made Easy Press, our goal is to bring you beautifully designed, thoughtful gifts and products.

We strive to make complicated things – easy. Whether it's learning new skills or putting memories into words, our books are led by values of family, creativity, and self-care and we take joy in creating authentic experiences that make people truly happy.

Look out for other books by Made Easy Press here!

Made in the USA
Columbia, SC
07 January 2025

51301776R00063